T0365331

La Cucina di Rosa

Cook Once, Eat Twice

Rosa Loretta Jordan

AuthorHouse™ LLC
1663 Liberty Drive
Bloomington, IN 47403
www.authorhouse.com
Phone: 1-800-839-8640

Published by AuthorHouse 04/08/2014

ISBN: 978-1-4817-0484-7 (sc)
*   978-1-4817-0485-4 (e)*

Any people depicted in stock imagery provided by Thinkstock are models,
and such images are being used for illustrative purposes only.
Certain stock imagery © Thinkstock.

This book is printed on acid-free paper.

authorHOUSE®

My idea of cooking is in large quantity, so there is always extra to make that second meal, this is what my book is about *Cook once, Eat twice,* so you still get that second dish while saving time and money. Also in some of my recipes I provided a way to substitute certain ingredients and still get that fantastic meal. Don't forget to check out the specialty and tip pages with all my little cooking secrets.

My past is full of family who loved to cook. My Italian Grandma from Italy loved to cook turning her home into a small restaurant where she would entertain people who love great homemade cooking. I grew up on a farm where times were tough, tomatoes and vegetables were plentiful, so I would help my Ma cook and jar sauces and jams for those cold winters. Those traditions I've passed onto my children.

Holidays were and still are big celebration with my family and friends stopping over for homemade food and drinks. I always enjoy seeing their expressions and when they asked what's in here . . . its delicious!!

Still to this day, my children and I have our Sunday Family Dinner. We get together, cook and discuss the weeks events. In our family we believe *A family who cooks together, eat together, stays together!* The recipes in my book are mine and my family's favorites. I hope you make them yours!!

Dedication

I want to thank my son Fran and my daughter Nikki for all their help and encouragement while writing this cookbook. And to my Ma, for my love of cooking. Special thanks to my good friend Ann Szymanski and my niece Sherrie Cox for their helpful input. Writing this cookbook has been the most extraordinary experience and lot of family fun and eating!

About the Author

Rosa is Self Employed and a Certified Personal Trainer, and when she is not Cooking you can find her in the Gym. She has two wonderful children who also enjoy cooking and spending family and vacation time together. She has a love for the outdoor and walking her golden retriever Sam. She was born in Pomona, California and resides in Southern New Jersey.

Aprons: Full Length Aprons in Red with White or Black print (La Cucina di Rosa) 65/35 % poly/cotton, ½ inch wide extra long tunnel-tie permits maximum adjustability of the neck loop. Center-divided patch pocket and pencil pocket. Machine washable, dry on low heat.

To Order Call 856-571-0400 accepting Checks, Money Orders and Most credit cards

$25.00 plus shipping/handling

Contents

Specialty Pages

Appetizers

Bruschetta

Preheat oven to 400

Slice Italian bread toasted

6-8 tomatoes diced, any tomatoes will do

2 tbsp. onions or scallions minced

2 garlic cloves minced

¼ cup olive oil, salt and pepper to taste

Fresh herbs chopped: basil, thyme, oregano, rosemary and parsley

Dice the tomatoes into small cubes, add the garlic, onion, fresh herbs chopped: basil, thyme, oregano, rosemary and parsley, olive oil, salt and pepper and mix all the ingredients thoroughly. Chill for 30 minutes. Very good topped on garlic toast: 1 loaf of Italian bread sliced and toasted lightly then rubbed with a peeled garlic clove and drizzle with a bit of olive oil.

*I like to pile it high on my garlic toast and top with my favorite cheese and eat with a lovely glass of homemade Vino!

Baked Kale Chips (Aunt Ro and Sherrie)

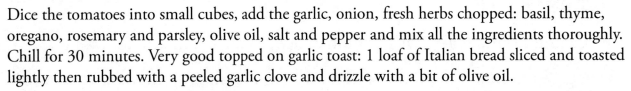

Preheat oven to 350

1 bunch of kale

2 tbsp. of olive oil

1 tbsp. of dried chopped onion

1 tbsp. of dried chopped garlic

Salt and pepper to taste

Line cooking sheet with foil, with a kitchen shears carefully remove the leaves from the thick stems and tear into bite size pieces. Wash and thoroughly dry kale with a salad spinner. Drizzle kale with olive oil and sprinkle with seasoning, mix well. Bake until the edges brown but are not burnt, 10 to 15 minutes, the chips will be crunchy. Serve and eat at once, sitting out will soften kale and lose the crispiness.

* To give a little Italian flavor, I use Wishbone salad dressing spritzers (balsamic breeze) about 5 spritzs with just 1 tbsp. of olive oil and all the ingredients above.

* Swiss Chard can also be made as a chip it has a butter popcorn flavor!

Fran's Crostini Basil and Fig

Preheat oven 375

Italian bread cut ¼ inch slices

12 fresh basil leaves

4 firm figs sliced

2 tbsp olive oil

1 whole garlic clove peeled

1 loaf of italian bread sliced and toasted lightly rub with a peeled garlic clove and drizzle the bread with a bit of olive oil, add basil leaves and a sliced fig and slightly drizzle with olive oil again, put back in oven for a about 5 minutes.

* Its winter time and fresh figs are not available no problem, you can use dried figs just soak them in warm water for about 2 hrs. they will come alive and plump use as directed . . . . Good Idea right!!!

Gorgonzola, Honey and Walnuts

Preheat oven to 350

large slices baguette

2 tbsp olive oil

6 ounces gorgonzola cheese crumbly

½ cup walnuts toasted and chopped

3 firm figs thinly sliced

2 tablespoons honey

Lightly brush the baguette slices with olive oil. Toast until golden brown. Mix the gorgonzola with walnuts and cheese in a small bowl. Spoon the mixture onto the baguette slices, return back to the oven and bake until the cheese melts, about 6-8 minutes. Top each with a slice of fig and drizzle with honey serve warm.

* This recipe calls for Gorgonzola Cheese you can actually use Blue Cheese very good substiute. I have used extra sharp provolone cheese in a pinch for arriving unexpected quest and it was still delicious.

Cranberry Walnut - Goat Cheese Toast

Preheat oven 400

10 slices of raisin bread cut in half

2 tbsp. melted butter

8oz package goat cheese log or cream cheese

1 cup finely chopped toasted walnuts

½ cup of cranberry relish and orange zest of ½ orange

Roll goat cheese log in toasted walnuts, wrap in plastic wrap put in refrigerator 1 hour. Spread the butter on the raisin bread and bake for 5 minutes on a cookie sheet or until lightly toasted, cool. Cut goat cheese into ¼ inch slices, spread toast with cranberry relish top with goat cheese add another layer of relish, garnish with orange zest.

To make cranberry relish: 12 oz fresh cranberries, 1 medium orange peeled and cut into chunks 1/2 cup sugar 1/4 tsp ground cinnamon. Put cranberries, orange, sugar and cinnamon in a food processor, pulse until finely chopped. Scrape into a serving bowl cover and refrigerate until ready to use.

* This is a great and easy snack, I always have raisin bread and small containers of relish frozen and if you don't have goat or cream cheese you can actually use what ever you have in the frig. it works!

Roasted Peppers and Ricotta

2 medium red bell peppers roasted (or you can use jar roasted peppers in olive oil only)

½ cup Olive

2 garlic cloves minced

16 oz ricotta cheese salt and pepper to taste

2 tbsp. Italian season finally chopped or dried season

Preheat the oven to 425

Set the peppers in a roasting pan and roast or place peppers on stove top racks turning occasionally until blackened and softened about 30 minutes. Transfer to a bowl, cover with plastic wrap and let stand for 30 minutes. Peel, core and seed the peppers, then cut them into 1/2-inch wide strips. In a bowl, toss the peppers with 1/4 cup of the olive oil, and half of the garlic, salt and pepper. In another medium bowl, whisk the ricotta until creamy adding remaining 1/4 cup of olive oil and garlic and Italian season. Mound the cheese in the center of a plate. Arrange the pepper strips around the cheese spooning the pepper juices over and around cheese, serve with crusty bread or crackers.

* This mistake I made creating another appetizer because a family favorite.

Easy Homemade Apple Sauce

3 to 4 pounds apples (gala, Fuji, golden delicious)

1/2 to 3/4 cup water or just to cover apples

Dash of cinnamon or nutmeg

Peel and Core and cut the apples into quarters or smaller pieces.

Place the apples pieces in a large pan with water just to cover and bring to a boil, turn down the heat and continue to cook until the apples are soften about 30 to 35 minutes stirring often. When the apples are tender mash down the with a potato masher, the apples will be chunky, for finer applesauce you can put through a food mill "I like my applesauce chunky" for extra sweetness and taste add honey, cinnamon or nutmeg.

* During apple season my family and I pick fresh apples and make delicious homemade apple sauce, I always make extra for freezing!

Baked Grapes and Kalamata Olives Spread

Preheat oven to 350

1 lbs. seedless red grapes

1/2 lbs. seedless Kalamata olives

3 tbsp. balsamic vinegar

3 tbsp. olive oil

1tbsp. Fresh chopped Italian herbs or dry italian herbs

1 small garlic clove diced

6 oz log soft goat cheese, or any cheese on hand sliced thin

Mix all ingredients together, bake in a shallow pan uncovered for about 2 hours at 300 degrees, stirring every 20 minutes, the grapes and olives will start getting soft and the mixture will thicken. Serve warm on the garlic toast topped with a thin slice of cheese.

* All I can say is OMG this spread is so delicious, great for family gatherings or entertaining, I always make a double batch because it goes quick!

Eggplant Appetizer

1 large eggplant peeled and cubed

½ onion diced

1 garlic clove minced

3 tbsp. olive oil

1 stalk of celery diced

2 oz capers drained

4 oz jar pitted green olives drained

6 oz tomato paste

6 oz water

Sauté's eggplant in olive oil with garlic and onions until soft, add the rest of the ingredients together and cook on medium heat until a slight bubble, turn heat on low and continue to cook and stirring occasionally for about 1hr or until very tender, should be thick. Served warm or chilled as a side dish or with crusty bread and a chunk of cheese.

* I remember this old family favorite when I was growing up it was on the dinner table a couple times a week. I recreated it over the years and we love it!

* What we do is make day ahead of time then served chilled on Italian bread as a snack.

Fran's White Wine Scallops wrapped in Prosciutto

1 lb. large fresh washed scallops

4 oz thinly sliced proscuitto

tooth picks

2 tbsp. olive oil salt and pepper to taste

3 tbsp. white wine

Salt and pepper each scallop, then wrap each scallop with a thin slice of prosciutto and secure with a toothpick. Heat the olive oil in a large skillet over medium-high heat. Place the scallops into the pan, and cook for about 2 minutes on each side. Once each side has been browned, pour the white wine over the scallops, and cook for another 1 to 2 minutes. Remove scallops from pan to serving dish and pour essence from the skillet over scallops.

* We don't only use as an appetizer but a great side dish with pasta and fish.

Ma` Rosa Italian Appetizer

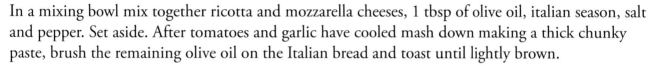

Preheat oven to 350

1 loaf of Italian bread sliced length wise and opened

2 tbsp of olive oil

1 pt. of roasted cherry tomatoes (see specialty's page in book)

16 oz ricotta cheese

8 oz shredded mozzarella cheese

1 tbsp. Italian season

6 slices of prosciutto

4 to 5 leaves of basil, torn up

Salt and pepper to taste

In a mixing bowl mix together ricotta and mozzarella cheeses, 1 tbsp of olive oil, italian season, salt and pepper. Set aside. After tomatoes and garlic have cooled mash down making a thick chunky paste, brush the remaining olive oil on the Italian bread and toast until lightly brown.

Now lets build it!! Spread cheese mixture on the toasted bread, next the tomato mixture bake for 10 minutes or until cheese and tomatoes are hot. Then turn on broiler now top with prosciutto and put under broiler for 2 minutes or less until slightly brown, garnish with torn basil.

* This recipes takes a little prep ahead time, but well worth it, this elegant snack goes great with glass of your favorite Vino or a hot cup of café!

Basic Hummus

2 15-oz cans of white cannelloni beans, drained and rinsed

1 garlic clove, minced

1 whole lemon squeezed or ¼ cup of lemon juice salt and pepper to taste

¼ - ½ cup of olive oil

¼ cup of fresh parsley or ½ tbsp of dried parsley

In a food processor, combine the garlic, beans, lemon juice, salt, pepper and parsley, mix until smooth while machine is blending add the olive oil until the mixture is creamy. Makes about 3 cups.

*For extra flavor I like to lace my hummus with (pesto, roasted garlic or roasted peppers) these recipes are in the specialty section of the book.

Scallops Stuffed with Pesto

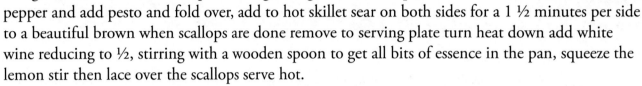

12 Big Sea Scallops (2-3 per person) salt and pepper to taste

2 tbsp. olive oil

2-3 garlic cloves crushed

¼ cup white wine

1 lemon

Pesto recipe on specialty page

Rinse scallops then pat dry, preheat skillet on high heat add with olive oil and garlic cloves, make a slit open leaving a hinge to the scallops, salt and pepper and add pesto and fold over, add to hot skillet sear on both sides for a 1 ½ minutes per side to a beautiful brown when scallops are done remove to serving plate turn heat down add white wine reducing to ½, stirring with a wooden spoon to get all bits of essence in the pan, squeeze the lemon stir then lace over the scallops serve hot.

* This scallop recipe is my favorite, the flavor from my homemade pesto and the garlic with the wine and lemon its just amazing!

Fresh Homemade Butter

1 cup of very cold heavy cream

1 ½-2 cup jar with a tight fitting lid

Make sure you have a slightly larger container for shaking room, put on the lid and shake up and down side ways for about 15-20 minutes pass around the table and keep shaking (its fun for the kids to make fresh butter) it will turn to a lump, but keep shaking, you will see it getting milky you're doing good when it starts to solid, drain then rinse and shape into a ball now wrap in plastic and place in the refrigerator to chill and firm . . . . enjoy!!

* We have made butter with our dinner quest, shake it then pass it, its fun even for the kids . . . nothing like making fresh homemade butter.

Roasted Eggplant Hummus

Preheat the oven to 400 degrees

1 large Eggplant cut in half long ways leaving skin on

1/3 cup of olive oil and olive oil for drizzling

1 15 oz can of white cannelloni beans drained and rinsed (you can use any kind of bean)

1 garlic clove minced

1 whole lemon squeezed or a ¼ cup of lemon juice, salt and pepper to taste

1/3 cup of fresh parsley or 1 tbsp of dried parsley

Place the eggplant on baking sheet cut side up, drizzle with olive oil and season with salt and pepper.

Roast for about 30 minutes until golden brown and tender then let it cool, scrap the cooked eggplant from the skin, combine together in the food processor eggplant, beans, parsley, lemon, garlic, salt and pepper, mix until smooth while machine is blending add the olive oil to until the mixture is creamy.

* Roasted eggplant is the way to go! One of my favorite ways to use up extra eggplants from my garden.

Nikki's Guacamole

2 medium riped avocado

2 garlic clove minced

1 lime

Salt to taste

In a mixing bowl mash the avocados with a fork, then add the rest of the ingredients stirring until combined. The lime keeps the avocado from turning brown then chill and serve with crackers, chips or veggies.

* my daughter Nikki makes guacamole quite often because we are always asking for it. We just love the special way she makes it with the perfect hint of garlic and lime.

Salads

Mozzarella Tomato and Basil Salad

4 fresh plum tomatoes

8 oz fresh mozzarella cheese or proscuitto wrapped mozzarella

8-10 fresh basil leaves

4 tbsp. olive oil

3 garlic cloves sliced very thin optional salt and pepper to taste

Slice tomatoes and mozzarella cheese same thickness, arrange the tomatoes, mozzarella, basil and garlic on serving dish, drizzle with olive oil, serve with salt and pepper to individual taste.

* I usually triple this certain salad recipe for family and guess, I like using the proscuitto wrapped in mozzarella cheese and extra olive oil for a little more Italian flavor, (as seen in my photo) serve with a crusty load of bread.

Arugula Salad with Balsamic Fig Dressing

6 cups fresh cleaned baby Arugula

6 fresh figs, stems removed

3 tbsp balsamic vinegar, dark

3 tbsp balsamic vinegar, white salt and pepper to taste

1 cup olive oil

½ cup water

1 garlic clove, roasted (see specialty pages)

½ cup shaved Parmigiano Reggiano cheese

½ cup toasted walnuts

½ cup dried cranberries

½ cup grape Tomatoes

Place the figs, balsamic vinegars, salt, pepper and garlic in a food processor and blend on medium until combined and the figs are lightly pureed. With the motor running on a low speed, slowly pour in the olive oil. Place Arugula in a large bowl, add dressing, walnuts, cranberries, and grape tomatoes toss to combine, top with shaved cheese.

* Its winter time and fresh figs are not available no problem, you can use dried figs put in a sauce pan and cover with water, bring to a boil for 5 minutes drain, cool, they will come alive and plump, use as directed.

Spinach Salad with Warm Pancetta Dressing

6 cups fresh baby spinach

2 large eggs hard boiled sliced

½ lb pancetta or bacon cooked and chopped

¼ cup balsamic vinegar

1 tsp sugar or to taste

1/2 teaspoon Dijon mustard salt and pepper to taste

4 large fresh mushrooms sliced

1 small red onion sliced thin

Wash, drain and pat dry spinach thoroughly. Place into a large mixing bowl and set aside.

Cook hard boil eggs, peel and cool, fry the pancetta or bacon and remove to a paper towel to drain, reserving 3 tablespoons of the fat. In that same sauce pan over low heat whisk in the vinegar, sugar, mustard and sliced mushrooms, salt and black pepper, heat stirring just to warm not hot. In the spinach bowl add the eggs, onions, pancetta and the warm dressing toss just to combine.

* We scrap the bowl clean when I make this salad and its so easy too!

Homemade Caesar Salad

1 egg yolk

1 fresh squeezed lemon

1 garlic clove minced

1 tsp. Worcestershire sauce

1 tbsp. dijon mustard

2 anchovy fillets

½ cup olive oil salt and pepper to taste

1 large head of fresh romaine lettuce, cleaned and cut into bite size pieces freshly grated Parmesan cheese

1 cup homemade butter garlic croutons (see specialty page)

In a large bowl, mash the anchovies and garlic until it forms a paste, add egg yolk, lemon, mustard, Worcestershire, salt and pepper whisk together. While whisking add olive oil and keep whisking until completely mixed. Place the lettuce into Caesar dressing bowl and toss a couple times. Sprinkle with Parmesan cheese, top with croutons.

*When entertaining, I make my salad in the middle of the table, my family and friends are impressed. To make a meal instead of a salad, you can add grilled steak, chicken, shrimp or scallops.

Brussels Sprout Salad with Black or White Beans

2 lbs. Fresh brussels sprouts

1 15 oz can of beans drained and rinsed

¼ cup of olive oil

Salt and pepper to taste

1 tbsp. dried chopped garlic

1 tbsp. dried chopped onion

Rinse and cut off ends and bad leaves of sprouts, cut in half and separate leaves. Drizzle with olive oil and sprinkle with seasoning add beans mix well. Served chilled.

Kale and White Bean Salad

Large bunch of kale

1 15 oz can of white cannellini beans drained and rinsed

¼ cup olive oil

Salt and pepper to taste

1tbsp. dried chopped garlic

1tbsp. dried chopped onions

With a kitchen shears carefully remove the leaves from the thick stems and tear into bite size pieces. Wash and thoroughly dry kale with a salad spinner. Drizzle kale with olive oil and sprinkle with seasoning add beans mix well. Served chilled.

* These two recipes are very similar, this is my way of making the raw salads but you can get creative and add peppers tomatoes, vinegar.

*To add hint of Italian and lower the calories, I use half of the olive oil in both recipes and use Wishbone Spritzers (balsamic breeze) about 6-8 sprays.

Soups And Stews

Potato Leeks Soup

3 large leeks sliced white parts only sliced

3 tbsp. butter

1 medium onion chopped

3 cups chicken broth

1 cup heavy cream

2 lb. potatoes diced in ½ inch pieces

Salt and pepper to taste

Melt butter in a large saucepan over medium heat add onions and leeks.
Cook, stirring, until onions are soft, add potatoes to saucepan then pour in enough chicken broth to just barely cover the potatoes. Continue cooking over medium heat until potatoes are tender. Using a potato masher, mash and stir potatoes, as you mash the potatoes and the soup thickens, turn down heat and stir frequently with a large spoon to prevent scorching on the bottom. Add one cup of heavy cream (or more if you desire) salt and black pepper to taste. Cook 15 minutes more over low heat, stirring frequently, then remove from heat and serve.

* This is one of my favorite soups to make. Very easy and tasty.

French Onion Soup with Leeks and Cognac

6 tbsp. butter

6 small onions, halved and sliced

2 garlic cloves minced

1 large leek white part only sliced

1 cup red wine

2 tbsp. cognac

1tbsp. Worcestershire sauce

1tbsp. Fresh or dried thyme

Salt to taste

4 cups chicken broth

4 slices ¼ inch thick French garlic toast (see specialty page)

½ cup each of grated Gruyere cheese and grated Pecorino cheese, mixed together

In a large saucepan, sauté the garlic in the butter until soft add onions and leeks cook on medium heat cook until brown about 30 to 45 minutes add wine, Worcheshire, chicken broth, thyme simmer for another 30 minutes until all flavors are blend at the end add cognac, stir. Fill oven-proof soup bowls ¼ of top from bowl add garlic toast, top with cheeses put under broil for 30-45 seconds or until brown and cheese melts. Carefully remove hot bowl and serve.

* I really shine here on my French Onion soup, laced at the end with cognac, this is a crowd pleaser.

Fran's Garden Fresh Veggie Soup

1 medium green pepper

1 medium red pepper

1 large onions

5 cloves garlic

1 medium yellow squash

1 medium zucchini

1 head of escrole

12 small okras

12 medium mushrooms

1 leek

6 scallions

4 stalks of celery

5 medium carrots

2 28 oz. cans plum tomatoes, crushed

¼ cup dried Guajillo / Chipolte chilli peppers, water to cover veggies black pepper to taste

Italian seasoning fresh herbs

In an extra large soup pot add all ingredients cut into bite size pieces, add water to cover, bring to a boil, lower heat to medium, cover and cook until vegetables are tender. Enjoy with a crusty bread.

* My son Fran love making this veggie soup its so full of flavor and good for you!

Minestrone Soup with Pasta and Beans and Vegetables

2 tbsp. olive oil

6 cups chicken broth

1 28 oz. can diced tomatoes

1 15 oz. can white cannellini beans, drained and rinse

2 carrots, peeled and chopped

1 celery stalk, chopped

1 cup onion, chopped

1 tbsp. dried Italian season

1 bay leaves salt and pepper to taste

1 medium zucchini, chopped

2 cups fresh spinach

¼ grated Parmesan or Romano cheese

2 cups uncooked tubettini pasta

Heat the olive oil in a large pot over medium heat, add the onion and celery carrots cook for about 10 minutes or until they begin to soften, add the garlic and cook 30 seconds, add Italian season, salt and pepper and the diced tomatoes, chicken broth to the pot and bring to a boil. Reduce the heat to medium low and simmer 30 minutes, stir in the beans, spinach, zucchini and pasta and cook until the pasta and vegetables are tender, about 10 minutes. Serve in soup bowls and top with the parmesan cheese.

*To use up left over pot roast or roast beef add to your soup with beef broth instead of chicken broth for a beefy vegetable bean soup.

Deep Dish Chicken Pot Pie

Preheat 350

2 cups all-purpose flour

1/2 teaspoon salt

8 oz cold butter or margarine

2/3 cup cold water

FILLING:

3 tablespoons butter or margarine

3 tablespoons all-purpose flour

1 cup half-and-half cream

1/2 cup chicken broth

1 teaspoon Italian seasoning salt and pepper to taste

3 cups roasted cubed chicken

2 cups fresh or frozen peas

3 medium potatoes, cubed

2 medium carrots, thinly sliced

1/2 cup chopped onion

½ cup chopped celery

Combine flour and salt cut in butter until course crumbly, add water, 1 tbsp. at a time, stirring until a ball forms. Divide dough into half. On a floured surface, roll out dough to fit a greased 2-qt. baking dish (deep dish).

For filling: melt butter in a large saucepan; add carrots, onions, celery, potatoes and chicken broth, cover and cook on low for about ½ hour or until vegetables are tender. In a medium mixing bowl add half and half cream and flour, whisk together well. Add flour mixture to vegetables, slowly stirring while adding. Add spices, frozen peas and chicken. Mix together, bring to a simmer, stirring frequently. Pour into prepared dish. Roll out remaining pastry to fit top of dish. Place over filling; seal edges. Cut slits in the top of crust to let steam escape. Bake for 20 minutes or until crust is a golden brown.

*A nice filling and warm dinner when its cold and snowy out. You can also replace chicken with beef, turkey great for finishing up leftovers just adjust the broth.

Hearty Beef Burgundy Stew

1 ½ pounds, lean boneless round or top sirloin steak, cut in cubes

1 tbsp. vegetable oil

½ tsp. Italian seasoning

2 garlic cloves minced

2 bay leaves

3 cups burgundy wine

2 ½ cups mushrooms sliced

12 small potatoes diced

6 medium carrots diced

32 oz of beef broth

3 tbsp. flour

1 medium onion, chopped

Dash paprika

Salt and pepper to taste

In a large soup pot, on low heat. Add olive oil, meanwhile in small mixing bowl add 3 tablespoons of flour, dash of salt, pepper and paprika, mix together. Coat meat with flour mixture. Evenly place meat in hot oil, cook until brown turning once, scraping bottom of pot to get cooked essence. Add rest of ingredients to pot, cook on medium heat until vegetables are tender, about an hour, stirring frequently. It will begin to thicken. Remove bay leaves and serve.

* This stew in make though out the winter months in my home with lots of homemade Italian bread.

Pasta

Roasted Vegetable Gravy *di* Rosa

Preheat oven to 350

1 large eggplant

1 large squash

1 large zucchini

1 large red pepper

1 pint tomatoes or 10 plum

6 garlic cloves whole

Olive oil

Salt and pepper to taste

2 tbsp. fresh chopped Italian herbs or 1 tbsp dried herbs

Cut eggplant, squash, and zucchini length wise, place on a cookie sheet, skin side down, add whole red pepper, drizzle all the vegetables with olive oil and salt and pepper. In a separate roasting pan add tomatoes and whole garlic drizzle with olive oil with salt and pepper also. Place cookie sheet and roasting pan in oven and bake for about 45 minutes or until tender, the tomatoes take longer than the others. Remove vegetables from oven and let cool, place red pepper in a bowl and cover with plastic wrap until cooled.

Once cooled remove vegetable meat from skin and place in food processor, add cooked down tomatoes with juice. Peel pepper skin and remove seeds. Blend on medium until smooth, add herbs. Heat and serve with favorite pasta dish.

* Save money and buy bulk on vegetables or grow your own . . . You can then double or triple the recipe and freeze the extra gravy.

Tortellini di Rosa

1 1/2 tbsp. butter

1 garlic clove minced

1/4 cup white wine

1 10 oz frozen baby peas, thawed and rinsed

2 cups heavy cream

Black pepper to taste

1 lb. cheese tortellini cooked and drained

1/4 lb capicola or regular ham sliced in strips

½ cup Parmigiano Romano cheese parsley for garnish

Cook tortellini then drain. In a medium sauce pan melt butter, add ham and cook until ham is slightly brown about 3 minutes, then add garlic cook for a minute or so until soft, add white wine while stirring. Then add baby peas, cream and black pepper and bring to slow boil for about 5 minutes. Stir occasionally. Toss cooked tortellini with cream sauce and top with cheese, garnish with fresh parsley.

* This is such an old recipe, and from making it so many times I have used half and half cream to save the calories and I still get the same richness and thickness in the sauce.

Pasta Carbonara with Pancetta

1 lb. Pasta

1/2 pound sliced Pancetta or Bacon

2 cloves of garlic minced

1/4 cup dry white wine

2 large eggs

1/2 cup freshly grated Parmigiano Romano

Salt and pepper to taste

2 tablespoons chopped parsley

Start pasta water. In a large skillet add pancetta, cook until slightly crisp,
remove and set aside leaving 3 tbsp. of grease. Add garlic and saut'e for about a minute, add wine
and cook until it reduces, about 5 minutes. Cooked pasta and drained, saving one cup of pasta
water, remove from heat, break the eggs into a separate bowl beat lightly with a fork, then add the
cheese, salt and pepper and parsley mix to egg bowl. Add drained, pasta and pasta water put back
into pasta pot and toss rapidly to coat the strands well. Add the pancetta and wine, toss again and
serve immediately. Garnish with parsley.

* Here's a thick delicious creamy bacon and egg pasta dish your family will love it!

Pasta Puttanesca

(An old Italian saying) Ladies of the evening, as they would place pots of this sauce by their
window to lure men!

1 lb pasta, spaghetti

2 tbsp. olive oil

4 cloves of garlic, sliced thin

4 anchovy cut into pieces

2 pinches of crushed red pepper flakes

3 tbsp. capers

½ lb kalamata olives with pits

1 28 oz can of crushed tomatoes

1 28 0z can whole tomatoes

Grated Parmigiano Romano

In a large skillet add olive oil, garlic and anchovies cook until garlic is soft and anchovies dissolve by stirring, add tomatoes, capers, olives and crushed peppers and parsley, cook to a soft boil reducing heat to low for 20 minutes. Cook Pasta saving 1 cup of pasta water, toss warm puttanesca sauce with cooked pasta add pasta water if too sauce is to thick, the top with grated cheese, serve.

* This is one of my favorite spicy pasta dishes, make sure you have plenty of Italian bread and VINO !!

Roasted Walnut Sauce

Cooked 1 pound fettuccine, saving a 1 cup of pasta water

8 ounces shelled walnuts, lightly roasted

¼ tsp. ground cinnamon

¼ tsp. grated nutmeg

Salt and pepper to taste

½ cup olive oil

½ cup heavy cream (I use light cream for less calories)

½ cup white wine

¼ cup Shaved Pecorino Romano cheese

¼ cup fresh chopped parsley

Place shelled walnuts on a cookie sheet, spread evenly. Place in oven and cook for about 5 minutes, stirring occasionally, watching they do not burn, remove from oven and let cool for a few minutes.

In a food processor chop walnuts until they are chunky but not to fine, reserve ¼ cup of walnuts aside, add the cinnamon, nutmeg, salt, and pepper, with the machine running, pour the olive oil, cream, and wine and pulse just to mix.

Cook pasta drain saving a 1 cup of pasta water then add your walnut sauce a little at a time and mixing well with ½ cup of pasta water add more pasta water if it is too thick, top with shaved cheese, parsley, and sprinkle with reserved walnuts.

* The Roasted Walnut sauce taste is unbelievably good, once you start eating you can't stop!!

* Also serve walnut sauce with steamed vegetables and meat dishes or serve warm on garlic toast (see garlic toast on specialty page) with your choice of cheese and a glass of chilled white wine.

Eggplant Parmigan Lasagna

Preheat oven to 350

2 medium eggplants

2 cups italian-style breadcrumb

2 eggs

½ cup milk

1 tbsp. Italian season

2 lb. ricotta cheese

2 lb. shredded mozzarella cheese

1/2 cup grated Parmesan cheese

1 pound provolone sliced

Homemade sauce/gravy see recipe below

Wash and peel eggplants, cut into ½ thick rounds, dip in egg and dredge in bread crumbs, bake the eggplant in the oven on a slightly oiled baking sheet until golden brown on both sides.

In a mixing bowl add the ricotta cheese, mozzarella, parmesan cheese, eggs, Italian season mix together well. Spread a ladle of the sauce/gravy on the bottom of 9x13 baking dish followed by a layer of eggplant, then cheese mixture continue to layer until you end up with cheese at the top add sauce and top with sliced provolone cheese. Bake until the sides are bubbling and the cheese is melted and golden brown, about 30-45 minutes.

Homemade Sauce/Gravy:

1 onion diced

1 whole green pepper diced

3 garlic cloves minced

2-3 tbsp. olive oil

I tbsp. Italian season

1 28 oz crushed tomatoes

1 28 oz can whole tomatoes

½ cup red wine

½ cup grated parmesan cheese

Sauté onions, peppers and garlic until soft add Italian season scrapping bottom of pan then add crushed tomatoes and the whole tomatoes crushing with your hands to a slightly chunky constancy bring to a small boil lower heat, then add the red wine and cheese stirring to mix well. I like to cook for about 1 hr then adding my cooked meatballs and sausage cook on medium heat for about 2 hours stirring often.

* I enjoy making eggplant parmigano "lasagna style" it just seems more personal for Sunday family dinners.

Rosa's Tips

* Slightly freeze meats before you cutting makes it easier to cut and slice.

* To thicken marinated add a cup of Greek yogurt this way the marinate stay attached to the meat for grilling.

* Leftover wines, freeze in ice cube trays, they can be used for any dish that calls for wine.

* The more finely garlic is chopped or crushed, the stronger its flavor, also let sit for a while before adding it to your dish.

* Rolling a lemon on the countertop (before you slice it) helps to break down some of the fibers and the juice will flow more freely when you cut it. You can also zap the lemon in the microwave for 10 seconds. This too will help the juice to flow.

* Fat from soup and stews can be eliminated by dropping ice cubes into the pot. Then stir and the fat will cling to the ice cubes. Remove the ice cubes after a few seconds.

* To keep poultry from sticking to the bottom of pan, try placing few stalks of celery in the bottom to act as a rack. This will add flavor and moisture as well when cooking.

* For moist and tender chicken submerge chicken breast in buttermilk for 3-4 hrs. in the refrigerator before cooking. If you don't have buttermilk mix 1 cup of milk with 1tbsp. of white vinegar or lemon juice.

* Substitute for a large egg in baking is two tablespoons of mayonnaise.

* Pre-heat oven meaning heat oven for 15 minutes before using.

* Blend almost any kind of leftover soup (minus bones) in a blender to get a sauce or gravy for vegetables or meat.

* To make bread crumbs, toast or completely dry out old bread / rolls and grind in food processor.

* Making Your Own Chicken Broth: Combine chicken scraps cover with water, simmer for 1 hour. Strain the liquid and use for chicken broth.

* Making Your Own Vegetable Broth: Combine water to cover all diced veggies celery, carrots, red bell peppers, onions and a variety of herbs and spices to make a tasty vegetable broth, simmer for 1 hour strain.

* Substitute for Fish Broth: Use 1 cup of clam juice for every 1 cup of fish broth required.

* Left over Chicken Broth, freeze in ice cube trays. In a pinch your ready.

* Left over Ham bone from Easter Dinner make a pot of hearty ham and bean soup.

* Left over Steak / Pork / Beef ,add to your tomato gravy (sauce) to enriched the flavor.

* Extra basil you can dry out for seaoning or make pesto for pasta and meat / vegetable dishes.

* Don't throw away brown sugar that's hardened. Put in a container with a slice of bread, it will be soft in a few hours, or microwave for a few seconds.

Chicken Cacciatore

½ cup of flour

Dash salt and pepper

Dash of paprika

3 lbs. of chicken breast sliced in 1/2 inch strips

2 tablespoons olive oil

1 onion, chopped

2 cloves garlic, minced

1 green bell pepper, chopped (optional)

1 28 oz can whole tomatoes

1 tsp dried Italian season

1/2 cup red wine

(Whisk together flour, salt and pepper, and paprika in a plastic bag, add the chicken pieces to the flour and shake until coated. Heat the olive oil in a large pot; add the chicken, garlic, onions, and Italian seasoning until chicken is brown on both sides. Remove the chicken and set aside, covered. Add the crushed tomatoes, scraping the bottom and sides of the pan, cover and simmer for 10 minutes. Add the wine, return the chicken, cook for an hour on low. Serve over hot pasta.

* This is one of my favorite chicken recipes served over pasta, the sauce is thick with the roasted garlic flavor, a must for garlic lovers.

Chicken Piccata over Pasta

2 skinless, boneless chicken breast, pounded ¼ inch thickness, cutting into 4 pieces

½ cup all-purpose flour

Dash salt and pepper

Dash of paprika

3 tbsp. olive oil

1 clove garlic, minced

4 tbsp. butter, divided

1 cup white wine

1 cup chicken broth

1/4 cup fresh lemon juice

2 tablespoons chopped fresh parsley

1 lb. pasta, cooked saving 1 cup of pasta water

1 lemon sliced in rounds for garnish

Place flour, salt and pepper and paprika in a plastic bag, add chicken pieces to the flour and shake until coated, heat olive oil in a large skillet, add garlic, cook the garlic until light brown, about 1 minute, remove the garlic and set aside, add the 2 tablespoons of butter with the olive oil, cook the chicken in the oil and butter until brown, about 5 minutes per side, remove the chicken from the pan and set aside, pour the wine into the hot skillet and bring to a boil over high heat, scraping the bottom and sides of the pan, boil until wine is reduced by half, about 5 minutes, turn down to medium heat. Stir in the chicken broth, reserved garlic and lemon juice. Stir in the remaining 2 tablespoons butter and parsley. Add the lemon rounds and cook for a minute on each side remove save for garnish. Return the chicken pieces to the skillet and continue cooking until the sauce thickens, about 15 minutes. Remove the chicken pieces to a serving dish with a few tbsp. of the sauce. Add the cooked pasta and some pasta water about ½ cup to pan with chicken sauce mixing well. Transfer pasta to serving platter top with the chicken and garnish.

* This chicken dish is a little time consuming to make but you wont be disappointed in the lemon chicken flavor.

BBQ Chicken with Caramelized Onions

Pre heat oven 450

3 lbs. of chicken cut up or thighs

2 large onions and sliced in large pieces

1 bottle beer

salt and pepper to taste

2 garlic clove minced

1 12 oz jar barbeque sauce or (bbq recipe see specialty's page)

2 tsp. liquid smoke add to bbq sauce

Place cut up chicken pieces in a roasting pan, pour the beer over the
chicken then add onions, garlic, salt and pepper, bake for ½ hour in hot oven, remove from over
and turn down temperature to 350, brush half of the bbq sauce on chicken, cooking for ½ hour,
then pour the rest of the sauce on chicken cook for another ½ hour or until sauce is thicken on
the chicken.

* I have had so many compliments on my bbq chicken over the years, the chicken is so tender it
will fall of the bone also a very smoky flavor it's like it was cooked on an outside grill.

Rosemary Chicken Fettucine with Sun-Dried Tomatoes

2 tbsp. olive oil

1 tbsp. butter

2 boneless chicken breast cut into 1/2-inch strips

3 cloves garlic minced

10 sun-dried tomatoes in olive oil, sliced thin

1 quart light cream

2 tsp. finely chopped fresh or 1 tsp. dried rosemary

Salt and pepper to taste

1 pound fettuccine

½ cup of parmesan cheese

In a large skillet, heat olive oil, butter and add chicken, cook until lightly brown. Add garlic and
sun-dried tomatoes, cook for about a minute or until soft. Add cream and rosemary. Scrape the
bottom of the skillet with a wooden spoon, stirring well. Simmer until sauce has thickened to a
heavy creamy consistency about 5 minutes, add salt and pepper. Cover and turn off heat. Cook
pasta, saving 1 cup of pasta water, drain and add pasta to skillet. Stir in cheese and ½-1 cup of
pasta water to thin sauce. Stir to combine, serve immediately.

* If you like creamy chicken and pasta dishes you will love this one, its very rich and flavorful.

Fran's Style Roast Chicken

Preheat the oven to 450 degrees

1 whole chicken, about 4 lbs

Inside chicken:

1/2 lemon

½ tsp. salt, fresh thyme, rosemary, oregano sprigs, basil and parsley

Outside seasoning for chicken:

1/2 cup of melted butter

½ teaspoon paprika

½ teaspoon Italian season

½ teaspoon garlic powder

½ teaspoon onion powder

½ teaspoon dried sage

¼ tsp. each salt and pepper

Cooking twine

Rub the inside of the bird with the lemon and salt, discard lemon, then place inside bird basil, parsley, oregano, thyme and rosemary. Using a brush, season outside of bird with ½ cup melted butter, sprinkle salt and pepper, Italian season, garlic powder, onion powder, sage, and paprika. With cooking twine, tie legs together. Place bird on a roasting rack on a baking sheet. Roast until the skin is golden and crackling crisp, 35 to 40 minutes. Reduce the oven temperature to 350 and roast for 25 to 30 minutes longer. Test the doneness by piercing the thickest part of the thigh with a thin-bladed knife. The juices should run clear. Transfer to a cutting board and let rest for 10 to 15 minutes before carving.

*We like roasting our chickens at a high temperature to give that crackling-crisp skin and deep flavor. We have found that placing the bird on a roasting rack allows the heat to surround and brown it evenly.

Spicy Yogurt Marinated Chicken Kebabs

1 cup plain Greek yogurt (Greek yogurt it thick)

4 tbsp. olive oil

3 tbsp. red wine vinegar

3 tbsp. tomato paste

Salt and pepper to taste

6 garlic cloves, peeled, flattened

6 tbsp. paprika

1 tbsp. cayenne pepper add more if you want it really spicy hot

¼ cup lemon juice

1 lemon cut into wedges for serving

2 lbs. boneless skinless chicken cut into long strips

6-8 wooden skewers soaked in water for about 2 hours (this prevents catching on fire when grilling)

Mix together paprika and cayenne pepper reserving 2 tbsp. set aside. Combine together in a large mixing bowl, yogurt, olive oil, red wine vinegar, tomato paste, salt, pepper, garlic, lemon juice and paprika pepper mix then adding chicken, cover and chill in marinade for at least 1 hour.

Prepare barbecue on medium heat, thread chicken pieces on soaked wooden skewers, throw out left over marinade, sprinkle chicken with reserve paprika pepper mix, brush grill rack with oil. Grill chicken until golden brown and cooked through, turning skewers occasionally, 10 to 12 minutes total. Transfer skewers to platter. Surround with lemon wedges, serve.

* My family and I love hot spicy foods and this is HOT! But it you want to cut the heat, just use less cayenne pepper.

Meats

Cracked Pepper Marinade of Beef

Preheat oven 350

3 lbs. London Broil

½ cup vegetable oil

½ cup apple cider vinegar

½ cup ketchup

1 tbsp. dried basil

2 garlic cloves minced

Crushed red pepper to taste

1 tbsp. cracked peppercorn, coarse

Combine all ingredients, excluding meat, together in a jar, shake well. Score meat lightly on both sides, place in baking dish, pour marinade over meat, cover and refrigerator for 2 hours basing and turning occasionally. Remove meat from marinade (save marinade for basting), place in baking pan, bake to desired degree of doneness about 45 minutes or so, turning and basting with marinade, turn on broiler and broil to a crispy well done top. Place beef on cutting board to rest for 10 minutes cut thinly on diagonal across the grain. Use the pan essence to lace the top of the beef.

* The combination of ingredients presents an amazing flavor, I usually serve with mashed potatoes. The next day the hot sandwiches of beef are awesome too.

Roast Pork Loin

Preheat 350

3 pounds boneless pork loin roast

3 cloves garlic, minced

1 tbsp. dried rosemary

1 tbsp. dried thyme salt and pepper to taste

1 12 oz bottle beer water

Place pork in a medium roast pan, pour the entire bottle of beer over pork, add additional water if needed to cover loin half way. Evenly spread garlic, rosemary, thyme, salt and pepper over roast, place in oven uncovered. Roast for about 30-40 minutes or until herbs are dried on the pork, then lightly baste with juice in pan, basting every 20 minutes, making sure herbs stay on loin. Cook until temperature is 170 on meat thermometer, approximately 1½ hours. Take roast out of oven and rest for 10 minutes, transfer to serving plate using essence to pour over pork.

* After dinner I place the pork in a separate glass container and essence in another then refrigerate. For the second meal slice the pork thin and add to essence that has been scraped of all traces of fat, heat until hot serve on a Italian roll with extra sharp provolone cheese serve essence on the side for dipping. See specialty page for long hot peppers recipe that go great with pork.

Crusted Blue Cheese Filet Mignon
with Port Wine Sauce

4 Filet Mignon Steaks (1 1/2 inch thick)

1 tbsp. butter

1/2 cup onion minced

2 cloves garlic minced

1 tbsp. fresh thyme chopped

1 cup beef broth

1 cup port wine

1 tbsp olive oil

8 oz crumbles blue cheese

½ cup panko bread crumbs

In a pan melt butter, add the onion, garlic and thyme, cook until onions and garlic are tender add the beef broth and the wine scraping any essence from the bottom of the pan, bring to a boil and cook until the liquid has reduced to about half, turn on low and keep warm. In a skillet sear filets on low until med rare turning once, transfer to a boiler pan then mix together the panko and blue cheese mashing to combine, preheat the broiler, and place the steaks under the broiler topped with the cheese mixture broil until the cheese topping is browned and bubbly 3 to 4 minutes, remove from the oven, and let rest for at least 5 minutes, spoon the warm wine combination over the meat and serve.

*I have made this recipe many times using sirloin steak instead of the filet mignon and has came out just as tender.

If you don't have port wine in the house no problem . . . . (substitute for port wine use 1 cup red table wine adding 2 tbsp. sugar).

Slow Cooked Baked Pulled Pork

For the Rub:

1 tbsp. kosher salt

2 tbsp. brown sugar

2 tsp. smoked paprika

1 1/2 tsp. freshly cracked black pepper

1 tsp. garlic powder

1 tsp. onion powder

1 tbs. yellow mustard

1 tbsp. liquid smoke

1/2 cup apple cider vinegar

1tbsp. chipotle peppers crushed

5-6 lb Pork Shoulder bone-in

1 12 oz bottle barbeque sauce or make your own bbq sauce from scratch (see specialty page)

Add all ingredients for the rub to a small bowl mix thoroughly, coat the pork with the rub massaging into the meat for about 3-5 minutes, wrap pork tightly in plastic wrap and refrigerate in marinate for 4-6 hours.

Preheat oven to 275 .

Remove marinated pork from fridge and let sit at room temperature for 1 hour, remove pork from plastic wrap then wrap in heavy duty aluminum foil and roast for 7 hours, checking and basing every 2 hours, continue to keep foil tight around roasting pan. Meat temperature should read 190-200 degrees and is fork tender, remove from oven, place the pork on a platter and loosely cover with foil, let rest for 1 hour before shredding, save essence and fridge. After resting use your hands or two forks to shred into chunks. Place the pulled pork into a large pot and place over medium low heat adding about 1 cup of essence after you have removed the fat then add the barbeque sauce, stir to thoroughly coat pork.

* The prep and time you put into your pulled pork will be greatly appreciated you will be the envy of your friends and family also good the second time around.

Fran's Mouth Watering Beef Brisket

5 lb. Beef Brisket trimmed

4 cups kikkoman soy sauce

4 cups sugar

4 tsp. minced ginger

1 large onion minced

2 garlic cloves minced

black pepper crushed red pepper

Bring to a boil soy sauce, sugar, ginger, onion, garlic and peppers don't boil over mixture. Remove from heat and cool completely. Add marinate to beef wrap tightly and let sit over night in the refrigerator.

Preheat oven to 300 degree, place beef in a roasting pan, wrap in foil tucking under rim of pan to seal in steam and juices. Cook for 4-5 hours until fork tender, remove from oven and let rest in the foil for 30 minutes before serving. Trim the fat and slice meat thinly across the grain. Top with juice from the pan.

* My son Fran's beef brisket its so tender and flavorful. Everyone wants his recipe!

Homemade Gravy with Meatballs and Sausage

1 onion diced

1 whole green pepper diced

3 garlic cloves minced

2-3 tbsp. olive oil

I tbsp. Italian season

1 28 oz crushed tomatoes

1 28 oz can whole tomatoes

½ cup red wine

½ cup grated parmesan cheese

Sauté onions, peppers and garlic until soft add Italian season scrapping bottom of pan then add crushed tomatoes and the whole tomatoes crushing with your hands to a slightly chunky constancy bring to a small boil lower heat, then add the red wine and cheese stirring to mix well, cook for an hour or so before adding meatballs and sausage cook on medium heat for about 2 hours stirring often.

Meatballs:

1 lb. lean ground beef or mixture of veal, pork and beef

1 eggs

½ cup milk

½ cup Italian bread crumbs

½ onion minced

1 garlic clove minced

½ grated parmesan cheese

Mix all together and make medium size meatballs, bake at 350 turning once until meatballs are brown on both sides.

Sausage: 2 - 1 lbs. packages of sausage mild or hot. Cut into links about 6" long and bake in 350 oven turning once until sausage are brown on both sides.

Cook your favorite pasta, dinner is served.

* This is an old fashion pot of gravy passed down, the aroma in my house is breath taking, serve with a loaf of homemade bread, salad and bottle of red wine. Nothing like leftover meatball and sausage for sandwiches the next day, or just freeze the meatball, sausage and gravy for that second meal.

Fish

Clam Casino *di* Rosa

Preheat oven to 350

2 dozen Fresh cherrystone clams

8 oz. block of Sharp cheese cut into ½ inch squares

1 cup minced onion

1 cup minced green pepper

12 oz. of bacon

* Buffalo wing sauce I use (crystal hot sauce)

Shuck clams and pull shells apart, place meat on cutting board. Set 24 shells aside. Mince clam meat and set aside. In a medium size bowl mix together onion and green peppers. Place empty shells on a large baking sheet. Evenly distribute all calm meat in all 24 shells, do the same with the peppers and onion mix, add a ½ tsp. of wing sauce on top of the onion and pepper mix, the thickness of the sauce will help keep them in place. Add bacon to all shells and top off with cheese. Bake at 350 for a half hour or until bacon is slightly crispy and cheese is melted. When they are done, remove from oven and allow them to cool for a moment, they will be very hot.

*Wing sauce

2 tbsp butter

12 oz Crystal hot sauce

1 tsp Italian season

1 tsp garlic powder

½ cup bread crumbs

Melt butter is a sauce pan and add rest of the ingredients except for bread crumbs, bring to a simmer and remove from heat. Stir in bread crumbs until thick. Let cool.

* Honest truth: when we have a gathering with family and friends I am always asked to make my Clam Casino so I make them!!!!

Cioppino over Linguine

½ cup olive oil

½ cup butter

2 onions, chopped

2 cloves garlic, minced

1 bunch fresh parsley, chopped

28 oz can whole tomatoes

1 bay leaves

1 tbsp. dried Italian seasoning

1 1/2 cups red wine

1 1/2 pounds large shrimp—peeled and deveined

1 1/2 pounds bay scallops

18 little neck clams

18 mussels, cleaned and debearded

Over medium-low heat in a large stockpot, melt butter and add olive oil, onions and garlic. Cook slowly, stirring occasionally until onions are soft, add tomatoes squeezing them into chunks then add seasoning and wine. Stirring well, cover and simmer 30 minutes. Stir in the shrimp, scallops, clams, mussels lower heat to a low boil cover and simmer 7 to 10 minutes until clams open. Served over cooked linguine or pasta.

* Be sure to have some Italian bread on hand for sopping up the delicious juices!

Roasted Smoked Paprika Salmon

Preheat oven 400

one and half pounds of salmon

1 cup orange juice

1 tsp. grated orange peel

1 lemon squeezed

1 lemon cut in rounds for garnish

1 tbsp. olive oil

2 tsp. fresh or dried dill divided

1 tbsp. brown sugar

1 tbsp. smoked paprika

¼ tsp. chipotle pepper

1 tsp. cinnamon

¼ white wine

Mix together orange juice, olive oil and 1 tsp. dill, place salmon in a large bowl add marinate coating well cover and refrigerate for ½ hour or more turning once. Mix together sugar, smoked paprika, cinnamon, orange peel, 1 tsp. dill and chipotle. Place salmon in a foiled lined baking pan, squeezed lemon on filets then rub the sugar paprika mix into fish. Roast in oven for 10-15 minutes or until fish flakes when touched with a fork. Let rest for 5 minutes. Transfer to a serving dish using a wooden spoon and lightly scraping the bottom of pan getting all the cooked bits, add the white wine, whisk and pour over the fish. Garnish with lemon rounds.

* I have never served my salmon dish without someone asking me "what's in here" the combinations of flavors; citrus, hot, sweet with a cinnamon twist you can't beat!

Shrimp Scampi over Pasta

1 1/2 lb. Pasta

2lbs. medium shrimp devein and cleaned

8 tbsp. butter

2 tbsp. olive oil

4 garlic cloves minced

½ cup white wine

1 tsp. italian season

¼ tsp. crushed hot pepper flakes

Salt and pepper to taste

3 scallions with some of the green chopped

2 tbsp. flour

½ lemon squeezed

In a large skillet saute garlic and scallions in butter and olive oil until soft do not brown, add white wine, Italian seasons, salt and pepper and crushed peppers, then add shrimp cooking for about 5 minutes or until shrimp turns a light pink, add flour slowly, stirring gently to thicken, add lemon juice. Cook pasta saving 1 cup of pasta water, drain add pasta to shrimp skillet mix gently now add about ½ cup of pasta water or more if scampi sauce is to thick.

* Double recipe for your family dinner and serve in a large dish garnish with parsley, great the second time around too.

Baked Cod Fish with Roasted Tomatoes and Kalamata Olives

Preheat oven 350

4 (6 to 8-ounce) cod fillets

Olive oil for drizzle

Salt and pepper to taste

Smoked paprika sprinkle

1/4 tsp. fresh thyme or ½ tsp. dried

1 lemon squeezed

1 lemon sliced in thin rounds

½ cup Kalamata olives

½ cup roasted tomatoes (see specialty page)

¼ cup white wine

Place the cod filet in a roasting dish, drizzle with olive oil and squeezed lemon then season with salt pepper and pakerika, now lay the sliced lemons onto the fish, add thyme, olives and the roasted tomatoes with juice. Bake for ½ hour or until fish is done when it is opaque throughout. Let rest for 5 minutes. Transfer to a serving dish using a wooden spoon and lightly scraping the bottom of pan getting all the cooked bits, add the white wine, whisk around and pour over the fish.

* Great dish for a dinner party, the colors are so nicely put together and the aroma will have your guest guessing!

Drunkin Clams

2 dozen clams

1tbsp. olive oil

1tbsp. butter

2 cloves garlic minced

½ cup onions or scallions chopped

1 12 oz beer

¼ cup parsley chopped

¼ cup grated parmesan cheese

Heat oil and butter together in a large pot add onions and garlic cook until soft, add beer and bring to a simmer then add clams cover until they open about 5-7 minutes serve hot garnish with the parsley and cheese.

*This dish can be served as a appetizer or a dinner over pasta, either way its so tasty you won't want to waste any!

Mussels in White Wine Garlic-Butter Sauce

Preheat oven 450

2 lbs. Mussels cleaned and bearded

8 tbsp. butter softened

4 garlic cloves minced

1 cup white wine

1 cup of fresh parsley chopped

Salt and pepper, to taste

1 loaf crusty bread

Mix together the butter, garlic, parsley and salt and pepper in a small bowl, place the mussels in a large baking dish, pour the wine over the mussels then spoon the butter/garlic mixture on top, cover the dish tightly with foil, and bake for about 15 minutes, or until the mussels open. Discard any mussels that do not open. Serve with crusty bread to soak up the delicious juices.

Delicious over pasta!!

Pizza

Rosa's Italian Pizza Dough

Round or square 14x12 in pan

2 cups lukewarm water

2 tablespoons yeast

5 cups all-purpose flour

2 tablespoons extra virgin olive oil

½ cup white wine (optional)

1 teaspoon salt

Add water and yeast to a bowl, let the yeast fully dissolve in the warm water for a couple minutes, add flour on a smooth work surface and create a well in the center of the flour slowly add the yeast-water mixture, olive oil, wine and salt, using a fork, bring the flour in gradually from the sides and swirl it into the liquid drawing larger amounts of flour in, and when it all starts to come together, work the rest of the flour in with flour-dusted hands. Knead until you have a smooth, springy dough. Place in an oiled bowl turning once so the oil side is up cover with plastic wrap sprayed with oil. Let rest for about an hour at room temperature or until dough has doubled in size.

Turn the dough out onto a floured surface and move it, by hand or with a rolling pin, into the desired shape and thickness. You'll need to keep your hands a little floury to keep them from sticking to the dough. If you're rolling out the dough, add a little flour to rolling pin, sprinkle dough with a bit of flour as it begins to get too sticky to work. Make sure your edges are a little thicker than the rest of the pie crust. Transfer to your greased pan, pour a little bit of olive oil and rub the entire pizza dough with your hands, add toppings starting with the cheese first.

Bake in a preheated oven at 350 degrees for about 30 minutes or until crust is golden on the bottom and cheese is melted.

Homemade Pizza suggestions:

Pizza pie: tomato paste, sliced garlic and a touch of Italian season (no cheese)

Fried Peppers and Onions: using wheat flour (no cheese)

Foot Ball: mozzarella cheese, pepperoni, red gravy

Ricotta Basil: ricotta cheese, tomatoes, red onions, basil

Pepper, Tomato and Onions (no cheese)

Veggie: Peppers, onions, tomatoes, mozzarella cheese, zucchini

Desserts

Basic Anise Biscotti

Preheat oven to 350

Mix the following ingredients together

2 cups sugar

1 cup soft butter

4 eggs

Mix the following ingredients together

1/3 cup brandy or apple juice

1 ½ tsp. Anise extract

1 tsp vanilla extract

Mix the following ingredients together

4 cups flour

4 tsp. baking powder

¾ tsp. salt

2 tbsp. Anise seed

1 cup sliced almonds

Combine butter and brandy mixture together. Add to flour. Form with wet fingers into 2-2 x 13 inch logs. Place on parchment paper covered cookie sheet. Bake for 30 minutes or until bottoms are lightly brown. Remove from heat and cool for 10 minutes. Slice logs 1 inch thick and lay on sides onto cookie sheet, cook for 7 minutes then flip. Cook for another 7 minutes. Remove from heat and cool on wire cooling rack. Best stored in cookie tin to maintain hard cookie texture.

* Other suggestions: toasted pine nuts, chocolate chips, cranberries, pistachios, raisins or any goodies in your pantry. Also a good idea is to dip the ends in melted chocolate for a sweeter taste.

Dolce Frutta (hard choc shell)

Italian Stuffed Cookies

Preheat oven 350

½ cup butter

1 ¼ cup sugar

6 eggs

1 tsp. vanilla

3 ¼ cups flour

2 ½ tsp. baking soda

¼ tsp. salt

Filling;

1 cup Apple butter

½ cup Apple sauce

½ cup peanut butter

½ cup walnuts, crushed

½ cup chocolate chips

½ cup raisins

½ cup any flavor jam

Combine above filling ingredients together. Cook on low stirring frequently until it forms a thick paste (about an hour). Remove from heat and cool. Whisk butter, sugar, vanilla and eggs until creamy. Stir flour, baking soda and salt together until well blended. Slowly add flour mixture into butter mixture until well mixed. Cover with plastic wrap and chill for at least 1 hour. Roll dough about 1/8 inch thick on lightly floured surface. Cut into 2 inch rounds. Place the rounds on parchment paper on cookie sheet. Top each with a rounded teaspoon of apple butter filling. Fold and pinch middles together.

Bake 8-10 minutes or until bottoms are lightly brown.

* You will want to double this batch, they got so quickly!

Italian Style Cherry Pie

Preheat oven 350

Two Pie Crust:

3 cups all-purpose flour

1 tsp. salt

1 cup butter, cold and cubed

6 tbsp. cold water

For the Cherry Filling:

5 cups pitted fresh cherries

1/2 cup sugar

2 tbsp. cornstarch

2 tsp. lemon zest

2 tsp. vanilla extract

For the Egg Wash:

1 egg and 1 tbsp. water whisked together

1 tbsp. water

Spray a 10 inch Deep Dish Pyrex baking dish with non-stick spray. In food processor add the flour and salt whisk to blend, add the butter and pulse about ten times, add the water slowly, and pulse until it looks grainy, turn out on a clean floured surface and knead into a ball, cut in half and cover with plastic wrap and refrigerate at least 30 minutes. Remove dough 5 to 10 minutes before rolling time. Roll out 1 pie crust on floured wax paper to an inch bigger than pie dish place crust in dish.

In a large mixing bowl add all the pie filling ingredients together and mix thoroughly. Once well mixed place in pie crust in baking dish. Roll out 2nd pie crust onto flour waxed paper, brush on egg wash. With a fluted pastry wheel cut ½ inch long strips lengthwise to make about 12 strips. Place on top of pie in a lattice design, any extra strips of crust add to your lattice, you can trim any extra crust hanging over, or you can roll up to make a lip for your crust, pinching the edges. If you have any left over egg wash, brush over handled pie crust. Place pie dish on cookie sheet and bake for 45 minutes to 1 hour, or until golden and bubbly. Take out and let cool. Cut and serve.

*I make this tasty pie from cherry picking with my family, nothing like a homemade pie filled with love!

Old Fashioned Chocolate Mayonnaise Cake Recipe

Preheat oven 350

2 cups flour

1/2 cup cocoa

1 1/2 tsp. baking soda

1/4 tsp. salt

1 cup sugar

3/4 cup mayonnaise

1/2 cup cold coffee (I use espresso)

½ cup sour cream

2 tsp. vanilla

Butter and dust bunt pan with flour, in a mixing bowl sift together flour, cocoa, baking soda and salt. With a mixer cream together the sugar and mayonnaise add the coffee, sour cream and vanilla, mixing well, add the flour/cocoa mixture to the sugar/mayonnaise mixture, and stir until completely blended. Pour mixture in prepared pan and bake for 30 minutes turning and rotating pan halfway through cooking time. Allow the cake to cool in the pan for 10 minutes, then turn out onto wire a cooling racks. Allow to cool complete before frosting.

Chocolate frosting:

1/2 cup butter

3/4 cup cocoa

4 cups powdered sugar

1/2 cup milk

1 tsp. vanilla extract

Cream butter until light and fluffy add coco and beat until well combined add powdered sugar half cup at a time, add milk and vanilla, beat until creamy and smooth ,scraping down the sides of the mixing bowl making sure everything is well blended now your ready to frost your cooled cake.

* Chocolate Chocolate!!!!!!

Baileys Irish Cream Cake

Preheat oven 350

2 cup flour

1 3/4 cup sugar

3/4 cup cocoa

1/2 tsp. salt

1 tbsp. baking soda

1 egg

2/3 cup coking oil

3/4 cup buttermilk

1/4 cup Bailey's Irish Cream Liqueur

1 cup hot strong coffee cooled (I use espresso)

Sift dry ingredients together. Beat egg, oil, buttermilk, liqueur, coffee together. Add to the dry ingredients; beat together for about 3 minutes. Pour into a greased bunt pan bake for 35 to 40 minutes or until tooth pick comes out clean. Cool cake for a few hours then dust with powder sugar.

* This particular cake doesn't rise to high, but size doesn't matter, because the taste is big!

Italian Lemon Pound Cake with Lemon Sauce

Preheat oven 350

1 ¼ cups all purpose flour

1 ½ tsp. baking powder

6 tbsp. butter

2/3 cups sugar

4 eggs yolks

1/8 tsp. salt

1/3 cup milk

2tsp. lemon zest

2tsp. fresh lemon juice

½ tsp. vanilla

Butter and flour a 5x9x3-inch loaf pan, cream the butter with sugar until light and fluffy, add the egg yolks into the creamed mixture. Sift together the flour, baking powder and salt, slowly add flour mixture to the cream mixture, add the milk beat well. Blend in the lemon zest, juice and the vanilla extract. Spoon batter into loaf pan.

Bake about 35 to 40 minutes until center is done but piercing with a tooth pick, remove from pan and cool thoroughly.

Lemon Sauce:

1/2 cup sugar

1 tbsp. cornstarch

1/8 tsp. salt

1/4 tsp. freshly grated nutmeg

1 cup boiling water

1 tbsp. butter

1 tsp. grated lemon zest

1 lemon, juiced

In large saucepan, stir together sugar, cornstarch, salt and nutmeg. Gradually stir in boiling water, then simmer over low heat until thick, stirring occasionally. Remove from heat, stir in butter, lemon zest and lemon juice. Serve warm over pound cake.

* My Italian pound cake with the zest of lemon is so refreshing on those warm summer days.

Dreaming Plums

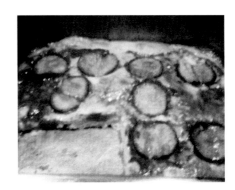

Sweet Pastry Dough:

1 1/3 cups all-purpose flour

2 tbsp. sugar

1/4 tsp. salt

1/2 cup cold butter, cut into 1/2-inch cubes

1 egg

1 1/2 tbsp. ice cold water

Whisk together flour, sugar, and salt in a large bowl. Using a food processor blend in butter until mixture has a grainy texture beat together egg and water with a fork and stir into flour mixture until combined well, knead mixture with floured hands just until a dough forms. Turn out dough onto a lightly floured surface and knead gently 4 or 5 times more. Form dough into a ball wrap tightly in plastic wrap, chill for 1 hour.

Topping:

6-8 plums, halved and stoned

1 cup of brown sugar

2 tbsp. cold butter, cut into small pieces

2/3 cup heavy cream

2-3 tbsp. vodka

Preheat the oven 400

Grease a 13" square deep cake pan, fit the sweet dough into the pan rolling out dusting with flour so that it covers the entire bottom of the pan. Press the plum halves, cut-side up, into the dough, then sprinkle the sugar over the plums and scatter the butter over the top. Mix the cream and vodka together and pour it over the top. Bake in the oven for 25-30 minutes, or until the dough is cooked and the plums are bursting with their own juices. Remove from the oven and serve warm.

* The sweet dough and the sweetness of the plums such a elegant dessert for elegant guess.

Apple Butter Whiskey Stuffed Biscotti

Preheat oven 350

Dough:

5 cups of flour

6 eggs

¾ cup sugar

¾ cup butter

6 tsp. baking powder

2 tsp. vanilla

Filling:

16 oz apple butter

½ cup coconut

½ walnuts chopped

½ cup mini choc chips

1 tsp. cinnamon

¼ cup honey

½ cup chopped cherries

1 shot of whiskey or apple juice

Combine above filling ingredients together. Cook on low, stirring frequently, until it forms a thick paste (about and hour). Remove from heat and cool.

1 egg white with 1 tbsp. sugar whisked together

Powder sugar for dusting

Mix together dough ingredients to make the dough, cut dough in half using one section at a time, roll out like a jelly roll using a rolling pin that has been floured to prevent sticking. Roll out to ¼ thick to 12 x19 rectangle, spread the filling mix on the dough, rolling and pressing down firmly to a long roll sealing at the seams, seam side down lay on a long greased baking sheet brush with egg whites and sugar , bake for ½ hr or until nicely brown, let cool completely, then slice ½" thick, dust with powder sugar.

* What can I say but yummmmmy!

My Brother Roy's "Thunder Road Burgers" and Janet's "Yorkshire Pudding"

Family favorites from Oklahoma

Thunder Road Burgers:

1 lb. lean ground beef

1/2 onion minced

3 cloves of garlic minced

1 jalapeno pepper minced

4 tbsp. ketchup

1 tsp. red cooking wine

1/4 cup cooked corn

½ tsp. cayenne pepper

½ tsp. black pepper

2 eggs

1 1/2 cups of Italian bread crumbs

6 slices cheese

2 slices of wet bread (place two slices of bread in a bowl and add milk or water, allow the bread to sit for a few minutes, soaking up the fluids, then squeeze with your hand to release fluids then crumble)

Mix all the ingredients in a medium size mixing bowl adding bread crumbs and wet bread, gradually until packs well, make patties 1 inch by 4 inches round it should make 6 medium size burgers then top lightly with black pepper and ketchup cook on medium heat, cook burgers on one side flip over reduce heat until both sides are brown, about 10 minutes, add cheese. Enjoy while hot!!!!!

Yorkshire Pudding:

Preheat oven 400

1 cup flour

1 cup milk

1 tsp. salt

2 eggs beaten

1 lb of bulk sausage

Form sausage into patties and partially fry, remove sausage from pan and drain saving about ¼ cup sausage fat add to a 9x9 baking dish. Mix together flour, milk, salt and eggs until smooth, pour into same baking dish top with sausage patties. Bake uncovered for 30 minutes.

Rosa's Basil Pesto

4 cups fresh basil leaves packed

1 cup parmigan cheese

1 cup olive oil

1/2 cup toasted walnuts or pine nuts

4 garlic cloves minced

Salt and pepper to taste

Combine all the ingredients in a food processor, except the olive oil, blend until a smooth paste, slowly add the olive oil in a constant stream while the food processor is mixing. Scrap processor put the pesto in freezer ice trays, cover and freeze for 2 days, separate and and put the frozen squares of pesto in a large freezer bag, take out as needed.

Roasted Tomatoes

Preheat oven 350

1 pt of cherry tomatoes (I use whatever I have from my garden, plums etc.)

2 tbsp. of olive oil

2 garlic cloves smashed

Salt and pepper to taste

1 tsp. Italian season

Mix all together and bake in a 9x9 roasting pan for about an 1 hour string once or twice until tomatoes and garlic are soft, and juice is thicken. Cool completely, add the mixture to a food processor and blend for a delicious sauce for pasta.

Roasted Peppers

Preheat oven 425

2 medium red bell peppers

¼ cup Olive oil

1 garlic cloves minced

Salt and Pepper

Place the peppers in a roasting pan and roast or place peppers on stove top racks turning occasionally until blackened and softened, about 30 minutes. Transfer to a bowl, cover with plastic wrap and let stand for 30 minutes. Peel, core and seed the peppers, cut peppers into thin strips. Add to medium size bowl, toss the peppers with the olive oil, garlic, salt and pepper. Chill before serving.

Roasted Garlic

Cut a ¼ inch off top of garlic bulb, place on a small piece of foil and drizzle with a teaspoon of olive oil then fold to make a pouch. Bake at 350 for a 1/2 hour or until garlic clove is soft. Remove from oven, cool and squeeze out the garlic.

Garlic Toast

Preheat oven 350

Loaf of Italian bread cut in half diagonal or cut in rounds

½ cup soften butter

1 garlic clove minced

1 tsp. dry Italian season

Parmesan cheese

Paprika

Combine in a mixing bowl butter, garlic and Italian season, mix well then spread the mixture on the sliced bread or rounds top with parmesan cheese and sprinkle paprika bake for 20 minutes or until bread is lightly brown.

Herb Butter for Meat and Fish

Serve this wonderful tasting butter with bread, or use to enhance grilled fish, meat, vegetables, or corn on the cob.

4 tablespoons unsalted butter, softened

1 tbsp. of fresh chopped herbs or dry herbs

1 tsp. garlic powder

In a small bowl, add softened butter and herbs and garlic mix together (for fish add 1tsp. of lemon zest).

On a sheet of wax paper, add the butter and roll it up to form a butter log about 3—4 inches long, twisting the ends. Place in refrigerator to firm. Slice as needed.

Homemade BBQ Sauce

6 oz. can tomato paste plus one 6 oz. can of water

½ stick of butter

1/2 cups ketchup

1/4 cup packed brown sugar

1/4 cup chopped onion

2 garlic cloves minced

2 tbsp. Worcestershire sauce

1 tbsp. liquid smoke salt and pepper to taste

½ tsp. of mustard

1tbsp. red wine vinegar

1tbsp. ground chipotle peppers or a smoky flavor pepper

In a large saucepan add butter, onions and garlic sauté's until soft, add the rest of the ingredients, bring to a boil over medium heat, stirring often. Reduce heat; simmer for 10-15 minutes.

Specialty Page 3

Roasted Eggplant, Garlic and Pepper Spread

Preheat oven 400

2 large eggplants

2 large red bell peppers

4-6 long hots for the hot spice (optional)

Salt and pepper to taste

2 tbsp. olive oil

Roasted garlic see above

Place clean eggplant and peppers in baking dish and roast for about 45 minutes until brownish skin forms on both, remove to cool then cut eggplant long ways and scoop out meat, remove the skin and seeds from the peppers. After garlic has cooled squeeze out the garlic from the skins, add eggplant, peppers, garlic, salt and pepper to the food processor blend to mix well while motor is still running add the oil, mix well until smooth. Chill for about an hour before serving.

Roasted Tomato Vinaigrette

Preheat oven 350

1 pt of cherry tomatoes (I use whatever I have from my garden, plums etc.)

2 garlic cloves smashed

2 tbsp. olive oil

1 tsp. Italian seasoning

Salt and pepper to taste

2 tbsp. red vine vinegar

Mix all the ingredients together (except the vinegar) in a 9x9 roasting pan and bake for about an 1 hour string once or twice until tomatoes and garlic are soft, and juice is thicken. Cool completely, add the mixture to a food processor and blend until smooth adding the vinegar while motor is still running. Cover and refrigerate before using, it will last up to a week.

Homemade Italian Croutons

8 slices bread or Italian roll cubed to equal 4 cups

1/2 cup melted butter

2 tbsp. grated parmesan cheese

1 tbsp. Italian season

2 garlic gloves smashed

Melt the butter in a sauce pan add the garlic cook until the garlic starts to brown around the edges 3 to 4 minutes remove pan from the heat and mash garlic until soft, mix the butter with the Italian season and cheese then drizzle the over the bread cubes. Toss until the cubes are evenly coated. Spread the bread cubes onto a baking pan in a single layer, bake at 350 or until croutons are a deep golden-brown, 15 to 17 minutes. Let cool completely

Printed in the United States
By Bookmasters